For Joe

May you Be
inspired to come
Book soon,

Best Wishes

Nov. 23, 09

The British Virgin Islands

A PHOTOGRAPHIC PORTRAIT

PHOTOGRAPHY BY

Mauricio Handler

Other titles in the Photographic Portrait series:

Cape Ann
Kittery to the Kennebunks
The Mystic Coast, Stonington to New London
The White Mountains
Boston's South Shore
Upper Cape Cod
The Rhode Island Coast
Greater Newburyport
Portsmouth & Coastal New Hampshire
Naples, Florida
Sarasota, Florida
Portland, Maine
Mid and Lower Cape Cod
The Berkshires
Boston
Camden, Maine
San Diego's North County Coast
Newport Beach, California
Wasatch Mountains, Utah
Phoenix and the Valley of the Sun
Sanibel and Captiva Islands
Asheville, North Carolina
Charleston, South Carolina
The Florida Keys
Maryland's Eastern Shore
Miami and South Beach, Florida
Savannah, Georgia

Also:

Artists of Cape Ann

First published in the United States of America by
Twin Lights Publishers, Inc.
Ten Hale Street
Rockport, Massachusetts 01966
Telephone: (978) 546-7398

ISBN 1-885435-17-7

10 9 8 7 6 5 4 3

Printed in China

All photographs © Mauricio Handler

Introduction and photo captions by Amy Ullrich, managing editor of *SAIL Magazine*

Design: Leeann Leftwich

The British Virgin Islands

A PHOTOGRAPHIC PORTRAIT

PHOTOGRAPHY BY

Mauricio Handler

GUANA ISLAND

GREAT CAMANOE

TORTOLA

JOST VAN DYKE

SALT ISLAND

PETER ISLAND

NORMAN ISLAND

ANEGADA

THE DOGS

VIRGIN GORDA

Table of Contents

This book is a celebration of one of the most beautiful groups of islands in the world. The images show the islands in many moods, from the hot colors of Carnival, to the splashy brilliance of their reef fish, to the myriad blues of the tropical waters.

GINGER ISLAND

COOPER ISLAND

Introduction

Wherever you are in the British Virgin Islands, there is something wonderful to look at. Climb or drive to the top of any hill and you'll be treated to a spectacular panorama of hilly islands, the tops of drowned mountains, rising from an azure sea. Stand on a beach and watch the water color change from bottle green through shades of turquoise as it deepens over a fringing reef. Go under water and you'll be surprised and delighted by the sheer variety of the corals and the colorful fish that live among them. Or go to the Baths, on Virgin Gorda, as most BVI visitors do, and marvel at what geology, water, and time can create out of strewn-about boulders. And don't forget to take a look at the tropical night sky, where zillions of stars twinkle in the absence of city lights and the Southern Cross makes a springtime appearance.

However you see yourself in the British Virgin Islands—sailing up the Sir Francis Drake Channel from Tortola to Virgin Gorda, reveling in the island-protected waters and fresh trade winds; relaxing on a quintessential white-sand beach fringed with palm trees or snorkeling over living coral reefs; luxuriating in landscaped splendor at a world-class resort—you'll collect memories and images that will stay with you for a lifetime.

So enjoy these images of a collection of small islands in a vast blue sea, produced by a talented photographer who has lived and worked in the BVI—on, under, and around its waters—for many years.

Calm Waters

What brings people to the British Virgin Islands—small dots in the vastness of the Caribbean Sea—is the water, in all its colors and all its moods. The shallows near the beach and over the fringing reefs are the faded green of beach glass; the middle depths are turquoise, perfect for snorkeling; the deep blue of the Sir Francis Drake Channel provides a highway for sailors.

Sir Francis Drake Channel

The perfect playground for sailors: Steady trade winds year round, a balmy climate with a rain shower or two to cool things off, protected anchorages just a few miles apart. And sailors respond—there are hundreds of boats available for charter in the BVI.

Sir Francis Drake Channel

The waters of the British Virgin Islands were once plied by pirate ships and trading ships, slavers, and His Majesty's ships of the line. Now they are highways for ferries, storehouses for fishermen, and cruising grounds for cruise ships and charter boats.

Rolling Surf

The trade winds blow from the east throughout the year—north of east in the winter, south of east in the summer—at an average of 18 to 22 knots. No matter what time of year you come to the BVI, there's always a cooling breeze—and a wind for sailing.

Sailing

Going somewhere? A charter boat gently
glides to the next evening's mooring.

Charter Yacht

Reaching along at a fast clip in the trades,
this charter yacht carries a crew to see to the
guests' every need—and then some.

THIS PAGE
Charter Boat, Sandy Cay
The view of the world doesn't get much finer than from the trampoline of a chartered catamaran.

OPPOSITE
Passenger Vessel, Road Town, Tortola
Every evening is a perfect evening in the BVI, balmy and breezy. The full moon is bright enough to block out the stars, and stargazing in an anchorage with no lights to block your vision is a treat.

Honeymoon Cruise

A newlywed couple plays at a scene from *Titanic* as their chartered boat sails in North Sound, Virgin Gorda.

BVI Regatta

The annual early-April BVI Regatta is the BVI's biggest racing event. Part of the Caribbean Ocean Racing Triangle series, it draws an entry list of locals and charterers for sailing and post-sailing fun.

Windsurfers at Play
Trade winds plus swells make perfect conditions for spectacular windsurfing.

Jost Van Dyke

Jost Van Dyke, from Tortola

Named after a Dutch pirate or, more likely, a Dutch planter, Jost Van Dyke lies a few miles north of Tortola. Once home to a Quaker community and to a number of plantations worked by slaves, this small island now has few residents but many visitors to its generous harbors, famous beaches, and equally famous beach bars.

Sunset, Jost Van Dyke

The sun goes down early and fast in the tropics, spreading a spectacular blaze through the sky. If you're lucky (and quick), you may catch a glimpse of the legendary green flash just as the sun disappears below the horizon.

Great Harbour, Jost Van Dyke

Great Harbour is Jost's main settlement. Quiet by day, it perks up at night when visitors flock to the restaurants and especially to the legendary Foxy's, where Foxy Callwood often weaves his guests into one of his calypso songs.

ABOVE
White Bay, Jost Van Dyke
Come to White Bay for a secure little anchorage and a beautiful beach with some great snorkeling. The Soggy Dollar Bar's Painkillers will cure what ails you, and there are hammocks on the beach for anyone in need of recovery.

LEFT
Millennium
Millennium at Great Harbour
Foxy's New Year's Eve party is always world-class. His party on December 31, 1999, topped them all, with hundreds of boats and uncounted numbers of celebrators.

The Beach at White Bay

White Bay's stretch of white
sand beach is a BVI classic.

OPPOSITE

Flying Cloud at White Bay

Built in 1935 as a training ship for the French navy, Flying Cloud served as a "spy ship" during World War II. She now enjoys an easier life as a member of a windjammer fleet, carrying vacationers through the Virgin Islands.

ABOVE

Kayaking at Jost Van Dyke

When your vacation home is a boat, your "car" is a smaller boat. Jost Van Dyke is a perfect place to explore or bay-hop by kayak.

Sandy Cay

Sandy Cay is one of four tiny islands off Jost Van Dyke that satisfy everyone's vision of a "deserted tropical island." But it's rarely deserted; the islet is popular for picnicking and for its nature trail.

THIS PAGE
Green Cay

A Hobie Cat flies a hull in the calm waters and fresh winds off Green Cay.

OPPOSITE
Sandy Spit

A catamaran stops by at Sandy Spit, another speck of sand and trees in the translucent blue waters of the Caribbean Sea.

Catamarans at Sandy Spit

Spacious, stable, and great for sailing with kids, catamarans have become a popular type of charter boat in the British Virgin Islands.

OPPOSITE

Kayakers at Sandy Spit

Use your kayak for exercise, for transportation, for sightseeing, or to poke into narrow, shallow, hard-to-reach places.

Nature

Barrel Cactus, Mosquito Island
Cactus is ideally suited to the BVI's
dry climate. Barrel, organ pipe, and
prickly pear cactus are familiar
sights throughout the islands.

Century Plants

The agave, or century plant, is hard to miss growing on hillsides. It takes ten years to blossom. The plant dies after sending up its 20-foot-tall yellow flowering spike. In its dried state, and painted and decorated, the century plant is the islands' official Christmas tree.

Palm Trees, Tortola

No vision of a BVI beach is complete without a fringe of palm trees, for shade and romantic good looks. You'll have to look in the forests for mahogany, bulletwood, and fig trees.

Orchids, Anegada

Wild orchids can be found in the western part of Anegada.

Botanic Gardens, Road Town, Tortola

You can see a wide variety of tropical flowers and plants, as well as plants of the rain forest, at the J.R. O'Neal Botanic Gardens in Road Town. Then head for Sage Mountain, where once-widespread native trees have been replanted, to get the flavor of a tropical rain forest.

Water lilies, Botanic Gardens

Beach, Cane Garden Bay
Sunset light casts a shadow over the beach at Cane Garden Bay, a place where music, dance, and good times have always brought people together.

White Bay, Jost Van Dyke
Coral reefs—many in the BVI are fringing reefs, which grow out from the shore, though there are also offshore barrier reefs and steep walls—help protect the shore and provide a habitat for fish and plants. The living corals on the reefs feed on plankton and help keep the waters of the Caribbean clear. Take a night dive or snorkel to see the coral feeding.

Small-Mouth Grunts

Reef Squid

Coney

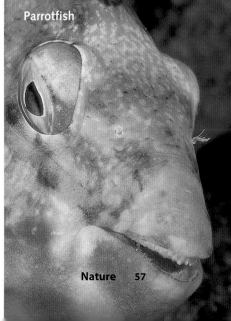

Parrotfish

Reef Fish

In addition to the hard and soft corals, the reefs are populated by a great variety of fish—over 100 species in the Virgin Islands. Some are coral feeders; some eat small organisms in the water; and some eat each other. It's not uncommon to see a couple of barracuda or a school of jacks waiting for a meal to swim by.

ABOVE

Cushion Starfish

Look for cushion starfish in sea grass beds.

OPPOSITE

Moray Eel

Moray eels doze in their caves during the day and hunt by night. Undisturbed, they are less fierce than they look.

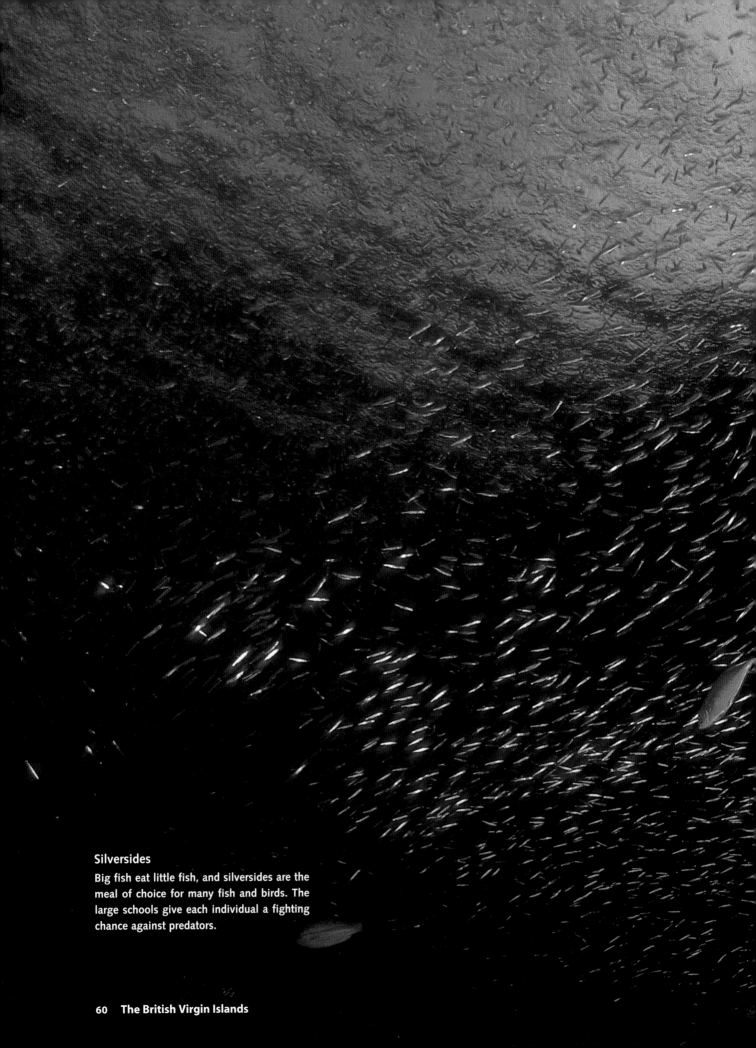

Silversides

Big fish eat little fish, and silversides are the meal of choice for many fish and birds. The large schools give each individual a fighting chance against predators.

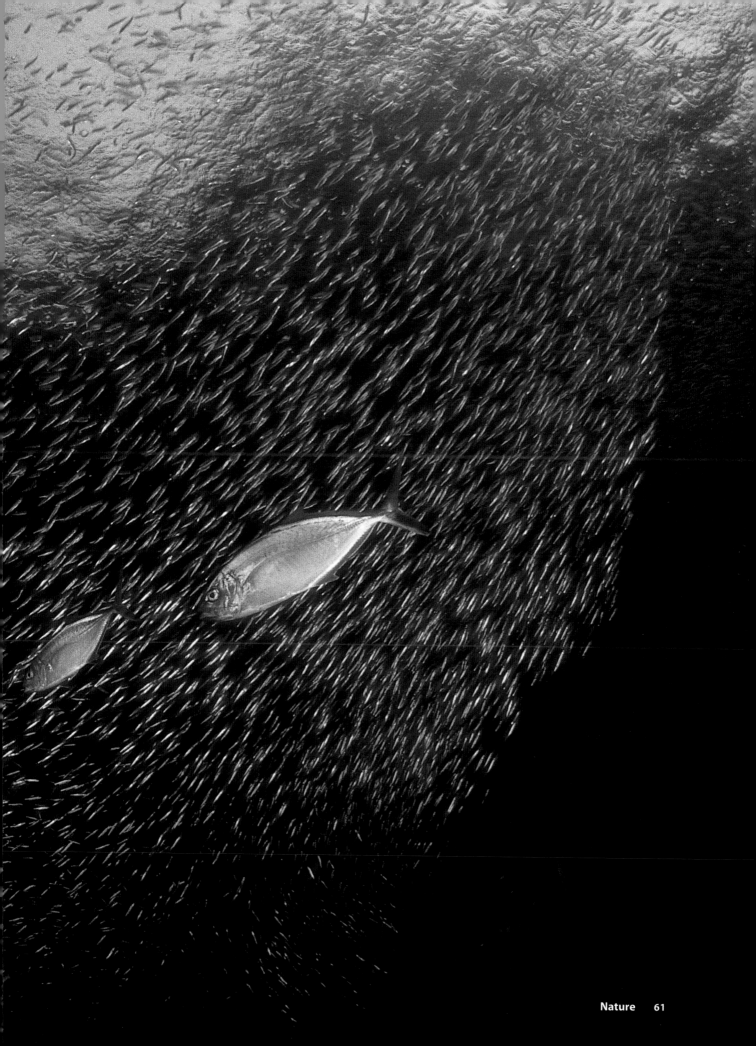

Pelican, Tortola

Terns, Anegada

Heron, Tortola

Heron, Tortola

Flamingos, Guana Island

Restored roseate flamingos are in residence at Guana Island's salt pond and on Anegada.

Iguana and Red-Legged Tortoise, Guana Island

The Anegada rock iguana and the red-legged tortoise have both been introduced on Guana Island. Anegada is the only remaining natural home of the ground iguana, which was once found throughout the islands.

Hawksbill Turtle

Much to the delight of snorkelers and divers, sea turtles are found throughout the waters of the BVI. The internationally protected hawksbill turtle shown here is still hunted locally for its beautiful shell and meat. All turtles lay their eggs on beaches, where the eggs are exposed to land-based predators; young turtles are favorite food for predatory fish and frigate birds. Man still remains the turtle's greatest predator.

ABOVE
Juvenile lizardfish

Mangroves, with their unique root systems, are important breeding and nursery grounds for many types of fish, including reef fish. Mangrove stands help protect shorelines, especially from hurricane winds and waves, and act as a filter that helps keep the water clean.

RIGHT
Agricultural Station, Tortola

Sheep and goats were introduced to the islands by European settlers. Seen from a distance, and without their distinctive cold-weather coats, they look alike—except for the tails. Sheep's tails point down, goats' tails up, except when it rains.

Tortola & Guana Island

Nanny Cay Marina, Tortola
Testimony to the importance of sailing tourism to the BVI economy, boats crowd the slips at Nanny Cay Marina outside Road Town.

ABOVE

Government House, Road Town, Tortola

Controlled by the British, who took control from the original Dutch settlers, for 300 years, the British Virgin Islands received a new constitution in 1967 providing for a ministerial system of government headed by a chief minister. The islands remain an overseas territory of the UK, with a governor appointed by the queen.

OPPOSITE

Residence, Tortola

Traditional West Indian architecture—hard to find in the islands these days—features elaborate gingerbread and bright pastel paint. This modern house echoes the traditional style.

Carnival, Tortola

Hot, hot, hot—and not just because it's August. The BVI Summer Fest, the colorful local carnival, celebrates the emancipation of the slaves imported by the British to support the plantation economy. Slavery was abolished in 1834, and many slaves became the owners of their land.

Tortola & Guana Island 77

Pusser's Landing, Soper's Hole, Tortola

Pusser's British Navy rum is produced and bottled on Tortola. You can't miss the Pusser's restaurants-plus-shops with their distinctive red roofs—and who would want to miss their generously sized piña coladas?

OPPOSITE
Soper's Hole, West End, Tortola

Charter boats gather at Soper's Hole, where pastel-painted West Indian-style architecture provides a home for attractive shops. Soper's Hole was the first settlement on the island— used, of course, by pirates.

SOPER'S HOLE WHARF
✦✦✦✦ HOME OF THE FAMOUS ✦✦✦✦
PUSSER'S LANDING

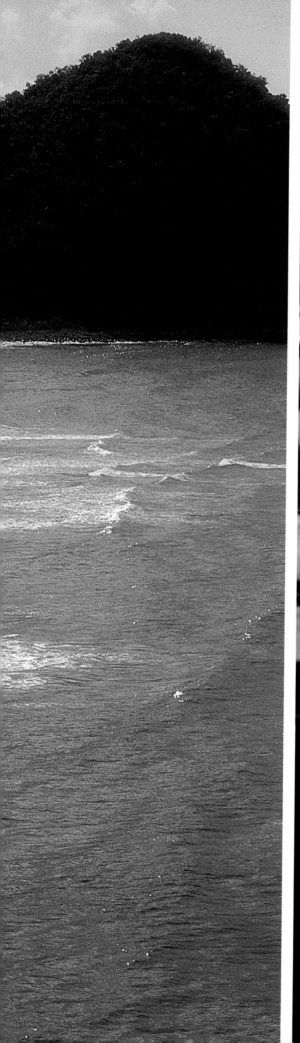

ABOVE

Bomba's Shack, Cappoon Bay, Tortola

Located on a popular surfing beach, Bomba's Surfside Shack is famous for its monthly Full Moon Party and Bomba's Special Punch. Constructed mostly of driftwood, the shack is occasionally blown down in a hurricane and quickly rebuilt.

LEFT

Long Bay, Tortola

When northerly swells are running, Tortola's north side has the best surf in the BVI. If you're a surfer, or just like to watch the waves come in, check out Long Bay or Apple Bay, where two well-known local restaurants—the Sugar Mill, for fine food; Mrs. Scatliffe's, for West Indian dishes—are worth a stop.

Tortola & Guana Island   81

Sunset, Long Bay, Tortola
Long Bay in a benign mood at sunset.

THIS PAGE
Brewer's Bay Point, Tortola

In the old days the British Virgin Islands produced considerable quantities of rum, from distilleries located at the aptly named Brewer's Bay, as well as at Baughers Bay and Cane Garden Bay (where Callwood's Distillery is still in operation and open to visitors).

OPPOSITE
Marina Cay, Tortola

Marina Cay, the subject of Robb White's *Our Virgin Island,* offers a small resort, its own Pusser's, and a good snorkeling reef. Located at the east end of the island, it's a great spot for taking photos, with a view of Great Camanoe and Scrub Island.

Trellis Bay, Tortola

Trellis Bay welcomes not only charterers but a number of live-aboards—people who live on their boats all or part of the year. If you anchor here, craftspeople will come to your boat with hand-made goods for sale; their works are also available at shops around the bay. Trellis is the home of *Gli Gli,* a replica Carib Indian sailing canoe.

ABOVE
Old Boats at the Salt Pond, Guana Island
Two old dinghies have come to rest at Guana's salt pond, where shore birds and flamingos congregate.

LEFT
Beach, Guana Island
Guana's beaches were made for walking. Although the island is private, all beaches in the BVI have open access.

Little Dix Resort, Virgin Gorda
Laurence Rockefeller's luxury resort at Little Dix Bay on Virgin Gorda, built in the 1960s, is widely credited with jump-starting tourism in the British Virgin Islands. St. John, in the U.S. Virgin Islands, is home to Caneel Bay, another "Rock resort."

Virgin Gorda &
Anegada

Nail Bay, Virgin Gorda

Savannah Bay, Virgin Gorda
The next bay north from Little Dix, around Blowing Point, is undeveloped Savannah Bay, a popular lunch stop for sailors when conditions are right. In the winter months the north swell rolls in.

Nail Bay, Virgin Gorda

Huge rollers come in at Nail Bay after an off-shore northwest storm. The west side of Virgin Gorda is the lee side and is usually calm.

The Copper Mine, Virgin Gorda

Nobody can say for certain whether the Spanish mined copper on Virgin Gorda as much as 400 years ago. It was probably Cornish miners, between 1838 and 1867, who left the remains that can be seen today—the chimney, boiler house, cistern, and mine shafts. Copper Mine Point, on Virgin Gorda's southeast corner, is a wild and windy place.

North Sound, Virgin Gorda

North Sound, also called Gorda Sound, is protected by islands and reefs. Ringed by resorts, beaches, and beach bars, its sheltered waters are ideal for sailing and water sports.

Bitter End Yacht Club, Virgin Gorda

The Bitter End specializes in water toys and sports—sailboats, windsurfers, rowing boats, motorboats, kayaks, diving and snorkeling excursions, and sailing day trips—and lessons in how to use them or do them. It's a popular anchorage for visiting sailors, and the last stop before Anegada and the open sea.

The Baths, Virgin Gorda

The Baths, at the southwest corner of Virgin Gorda, must be the most-visited place in the BVI, if not the entire Caribbean. Everyone comes to marvel at the huge boulders, to walk through the inner grottoes illuminated by shafts of light, and to enjoy the large interior pools of warm water. For a private moment, come early or stay late.

Boulders, the Baths

The boulders at the Baths are volcanic, formed of a hard quartz granite known as diorite. The hardness of the material probably accounts for the fact that they haven't eroded away, even though they've been in place for 60 million years.

The Baths

The Baths attract swimmers and snorkelers as well as explorers and rock climbers. Around to the south is Devil's Bay, accessible by walking trail or by snorkeling around the point that separates the bay from the Baths.

Pomato Point, Anegada

Anegada, the "drowned island," is famous for its reefs (a hiding place for pirates), its wrecks (a result of the maze of reefs), and its lobsters. The only coral island in the BVI, Anegada is only 28 feet at its highest point. Pomato Point is a landmark for sailors seeking a safe entry into the harbor on the south side.

Lobstermen, Anegada

Anegada lobster is renowned throughout the islands. Fishermen pull into the docks with their catch every day.

North-Side Beach, Anegada

Anegada's north-side beaches offer superb snorkeling, diving, and beachcombing. Loblolly Bay, named for the loblolly tree, is the best known, for its extraordinary undersea life.

Salt Island

Salt Island once provided salt, important as a preservative as well as a seasoning, for the British Royal Navy; it was collected by island residents in the spring, when the three interior salt ponds evaporated. Now the island population is down to a caretaker or two, but salt is still collected and sold to visitors, and the governor still collects the Crown's annual rent—a bag of salt.

Other Islands

NORMAN, PETER, SALT, COOPER AND GINGER

ABOVE

Diver at the *Rhone*

The 310-foot Royal Mail Steamer Rhone went down off Salt Island in an 1867 hurricane, with the loss of all hands. The remarkably well preserved wreck lies in 20 to 80 feet of water and is probably the most popular dive site in the BVI. On a calm day, snorkelers too can get a clear view of the ship.

OPPOSITE

Ginger Island

Though divers head for nearby Alice in Wonderland, Ginger Island has a small bay inside a reef. Ginger has few human visitors, but in May the island comes alive with nesting birds.

Cooper Island

Cooper Island was made for snorkelers. Manchioneel Bay offers a beautiful palm tree-fringed sandy beach, a stretch of sea grass to explore (watch for grazing green turtles and rays), and super snorkeling (also a great shallow dive) at Cistern Point.

Cooper Island Beach Club
Aside from this small hotel, Cooper Island is uninhabited. The beach bar, popular with sailors, is one of those places rumored to have been the inspiration for Jimmy Buffett's "Cheeseburgers in Paradise"—but the BVI has many inspiring beach bars.

ABOVE

The Indians

The Indians—four pinnacles that remind some people of the feathers on an Indian war bonnet—and nearby Pelican Island are a dinghy ride from The Bight on Norman Island. There's something here for every diver and snorkeler: a steep walled canyon, a tunnel (swim through if you dare!), a small cave, ledges, and coral shallows. Come at sun-up, when there's nobody here but the fish.

OPPOSITE

Boats at The Indians

Visiting sailboats and dinghies at The Indians tie up to moorings installed by the National Parks Trust; the system was designed by Dr. John Halas and is used in reef areas worldwide. The moorings protect the fragile reefs and prevent damage from careless anchoring. Moorings have been installed in popular anchorages and at snorkel/dive sites throughout the British Virgin Islands.

Peter Island Resort
Privately owned Peter Island Resort is a short ferry ride across the Sir Francis Drake Channel from Road Town. Many sailors overnight in Sprat Bay, the entrance to the resort from the sea. Local fishermen cast their nets into the bay at Great Harbour in the afternoon.

Deadman's Bay

Most often used as a day anchorage by visiting sailors, Deadman's Bay offers seagrass beds and resident sea turtles for snorkelers and a world-class, mile-long sandy beach for strollers and sun lovers. The story goes that the bay is named after the dead bodies of sailors; they were marooned on Dead Chest Island by the pirate Blackbeard and died when they tried to swim across.

ABOVE
Key Cay

Despite the large number of sailors who come to the BVI year round, it's still possible to find a secluded anchorage—if you know where to look. Key Cay lies off Key Point, on the south side of Peter Island, and rarely draws a crowd.

BELOW
Norman Island

Legends of buried pirate treasure—to say nothing of a couple of great anchorages and superb snorkeling—bring visitors to Norman Island, which is said to have been named after a pirate. The Bight, on the island's western corner, is one of the most popular anchorages in the Virgin Islands; on the other side of Treasure Point are the famous caves, which may (or may not) be where the treasure is buried. Spy Glass Hill, on the north side, would have been a handy observation point for pirates keeping a lookout for treasure galleons.

ABOVE LEFT
The Caves

The Caves have unburied treasure for snorkelers. Shallow inside, each extends back into the body of the island. Bring an underwater flashlight to get a good view of the brilliantly colored algae, sponges, and encrusting corals on the walls just below the surface.

LEFT
Rays of Light, the Caves

The southernmost cave has a natural skylight that illuminates the water below.

RIGHT
Snorkeler, the Caves

Snorkeling at the Caves can put you inside a cloud of sergeant majors with their characteristic black stripes. Schooling bait fish beneath the surge bring laughing gulls and pelicans, eager for an easy-to-catch meal.

BELOW RIGHT
The "Willie T"

Named for William Thornton, the designer of the U.S. capitol, a native of Jost Van Dyke, the "Willie T," a replica Nova Scotia topsail schooner, is a long-time fixture in the Bight. It serves up lunch, dinner, and legendary parties.

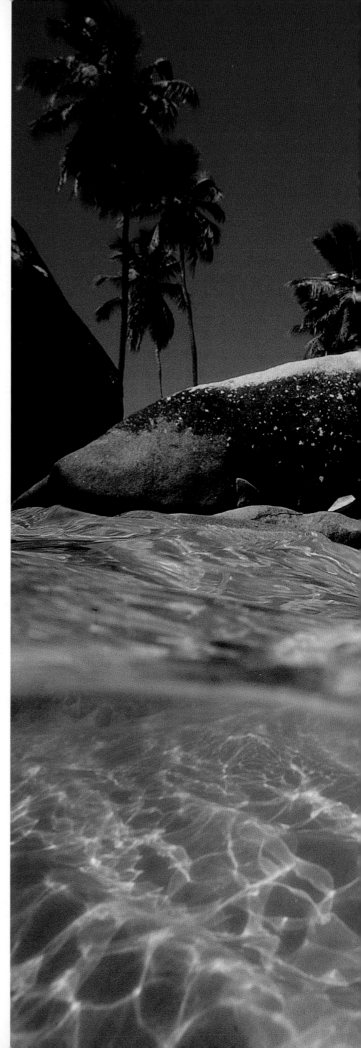

Dedication

I dedicate this, my first book, to my family—my wife, Michele, my twin daughters, Maya and Taylor, my grandmother Marta, my mother, Sonia, my sister, Andrea, and my uncle, Pancho—all of whom have been a source of strength and inspiration.

Mauricio Handler

Acknowledgements

Photography is a slow personal process developed over many years. It involves large amounts of equipment, extensive patience, and, most of all, experiences. Since arriving in the British Virgin Islands in 1985, I have had many such great experiences and met many wonderful people who have, in one way or another, influenced my photography, my work, and my life. It is those who have shared the wonderful moments that make up the BVI experience I would like to thank here.

To Michael and Marietta Satz, who believed in me for so many years and entrusted me with their precious yacht, Pancha, I will forever be in your debt. To my very special friend Paulina Dean, with whom I have traveled to the ends of the earth, I thank you from the depth of my heart for your great vision and encouragement. To my good friend Chris Tilling, who has also lived for many years in the islands dreaming of images to be made, thanks for listening. And to my old friends Randy and Maritha Keil, who in many ways inspired me to embark on this quest for images in the first place.